CREATING THE WORLD F

Jakob von Uexkull is the founder and president of the World Future Council Initiative. He is also founder of Right Livelihood Award, and past Member of the European Parliament. From 1987 to 1989 he was a member of the Delegation for Relations with the Supreme Soviet of the USSR. He is a former trustee of the New Economics Foundation, London, a patron of Friends of the Earth International, and a member of the Global Commission to Fund the United Nations. He has served on the Board of Greenpeace, Germany, and is on the Council of Governance of Transparency International. He lectures widely on sustainable development and peace issues.

Prof. Herbert Girardet is an author, consultant and filmmaker, and director of research of the World Future Council Initiative. He is chairman of the Schumacher Society, UK, an honorary fellow of the RIBA, a patron of the Soil Association, and a UN Global 500 Award recipient. His eight books include *The Gaia Atlas of Cities* (1992), *Creating Sustainable Cities* (1999), and *Cities, People, Planet* (2004). He has produced 50 TV documentaries on sustainable development. In 2003 he was 'Thinker in Residence' in Adelaide, developing sustainability strategies for South Australia. He is visiting professor at the University of Northumbria, Middlesex University and the University of West of England.

World **Future** Council

Creating the
World Future Council

Jakob von Uexkull and Herbert Girardet

PUBLISHED BY GREEN BOOKS

FOR THE WORLD FUTURE COUNCIL INITIATIVE

First published in 2004
by Green Books Ltd
Foxhole, Dartington,
Totnes, Devon TQ9 6EB
www.greenbooks.co.uk
info@greenbooks.co.uk

for The World Future Council Initiative
Trafalgar House, 11 Waterloo Place, London SW1Y 4AU
Tel: 020 7863 8833   Fax: 020 7839 5162
info.uk@worldfuture council.org
www.worldfuture council.org

See website for details of offices in Germany and the USA

Cover design by Rick Lawrence

Printed by J. W. Arrowsmith Ltd, Bristol, UK

Text printed on Corona Offset 100% recycled paper
Cover board made from 80% recycled materials

A catalogue record for this publication
is available from the British Library

ISBN 1 903998 46 8

Contents

This summarizes the need to create a new international organization
that views the world from an ethical perspective. The World Future
Council will be an independent body that injects a missing ethical
dimension into the conduct of national and international affairs. It
will set up 24 expert commissions on key environmental, political,
economic and social issues. Its key premise is not that there is a 'values
vacuum', but that widely agreed values are not being acted upon.

This second part of the book is a short history of efforts by the
international community to address some key issues of our time—
pollution, deforestation, climate change, poverty, injustice, and lack of
action on sustainability. The gap between where we are and where we
need to be is actually growing rather than getting smaller. The World
Future Council will address these issues, challenging civil society,
governments and the UN to a new sense of urgency.

The 24 commissions will be concerned with the quest for sustainability,
justice and peace. This section summarises the proposed commissions
in short paragraphs and sets out their work programmes over the
coming years.

"It could be worthwhile to establish a body whose principle task would be to monitor human affairs from the perspective of ethics. . . . This would consist of an elected group of individuals drawn . . . from a wide variety of backgrounds. . . . Because this body would not actually be invested with political power, its pronouncements would not be legally binding. But by virtue of its independence . . . these deliberations would be seen to represent the conscience of the world. They would thus carry moral authority."

—His Holiness, The Dalai Lama

Introduction:

The World Future Council —Values, Vision, Solutions

In today's world, the short-term gain of a few has become more important than the long-term well-being of people and planet. It is this kind of wilful short-sightedness that has helped global commerce hijack our intrinsic human values.

We need to hear from people inspired by ethics, experience and wisdom who know how to make the connections between the many complex problems facing us.

A group of thinkers and activists from around the world are now working to create the World Future Council, a new global institution that will speak out about the things that are essential for a viable future – sustainability, peace and justice.

What will it do? The Council will address important environment, peace, governance, human development and human rights issues by encouraging the implementation and enforcement of treaties and laws. When needed, it will commission research and recommend new policies and laws to protect the welfare of the planet and its citizens.

The Council, made up of 100 globally recognized wise elders, pioneers and youth leaders, will work with decision-makers to provide direction for a sustainable future. The Council will consider and publicize its proposals for action at annual meetings that will be broadcast worldwide.

Will anyone listen? Mere pronouncements from even an ethical group like this one will not create a better world. Recommendations from the World Future Council must reach and influence policy-makers as they allocate funds and enact and enforce both national and international laws.

The Council will work closely with national legislators from all over the world to develop step-by-step reforms and legislation to overcome the current 'implementation gap'. The EarthAction Network, with its 2,200 Partner Organizations in more than 160 countries, will build global support for the Council's recommendations.

How will it work? Much of the World Future Council's work will happen in smaller Commissions oriented around specific issues. Civil society organizations, UN agencies, cities and others will be invited to help organize and sponsor individual Commissions, each with its own focus. Every Commission will engage the world's leading experts in the field, who will conduct research, hold hearings and publish reports with policy recommendations for the Council's consideration and action.

What does it stand for? The Council will represent the shared ethical values of citizens worldwide. The Council's considerations will be partly based on existing initiatives like the Earth Charter and international treaties that are the result of lengthy and detailed global consultative processes.

In many areas we already know what needs to be done, but policy-makers fail to act—due to political cowardice, short-sightedness and corruption. In these cases, the World Future Council will focus on closing this 'action gap' between what is being done and what urgently needs to be done. In other areas, additional research will be carried out to develop new, innovative proposals.

How can you help? If you are interested in supporting the World Future Council Initiative, please get in touch. A response form can be read and filled out electronically in English, French, Spanish or German on our Web site: www.worldfuturecouncil.org.

Or get in touch with our WFC offices:

World Future Council
Trafalgar House, Room 414
11 Waterloo Place
London SW1Y 4AU
UK
Tel: +44 20 7863 8833 Fax: +44 20 7839 5162
Email: info.uk@worldfuturecouncil.org

World Future Council
30 Cottage Street
Amherst
MA 01002
USA
Tel: +1 413 549 8118 Fax: +1 413 549 0544
Email: info.usa@worldfuturecouncil.org

World Future Council
Haus der Zukunft
Osterstrasse 58
20259 Hamburg
Germany
Tel: +49 40 4907 1100 Fax: +49 40 4907 1199
Email: info@weltzukunftsrat.de

Making it happen

by Jakob von Uexkull

Global Values and Global Stability

At the start of the new millennium the world needs an independent body to inject a missing ethical dimension into the conduct of national and global affairs. We need a clear and sustained voice that expresses our values as world citizens, rather than just as global consumers. Our key challenge is not a 'values vacuum', but that widely agreed values are not being acted on.

The **World Future Council** (WFC) is being set up to ensure that ethical, long-term thinking becomes central to the debate about our common future.

The challenges that humanity now faces are historically unique, both in their globality and their vast time horizon. For the first time in our history we are not just affecting the next 100 years by what we decide—or don't decide—today, but millennial or even geological time spans. We have the power to severely affect present and future generations, yet we seem incapable of dealing with the global and long-term impacts of our actions. The integrity of our planet is being damaged by the impacts of a global consumer society, yet despite the growing clamour for change, alternatives are rarely explored, leaving many of us feeling increasingly angry and frustrated.

We simultaneously celebrate and lament our 'mastery' over nature. We seem to be part of some automatic, seemingly unsteerable process called progress, but our modern experiment of putting scientific and economic freedom first, and then bringing in ethics to deal with the consequences, is not working.

Our greatest problem is not poverty, environmental collapse or terrorism—it is our failure to respond to the great challenges of our time, despite having the knowledge and power to do so.

The World Future Council aims to rise to this challenge. It seeks to be a powerful global voice that appeals and responds to our basic human values.

The power of the Council will be primarily ethical—but its significance should not be underestimated. As a voice of Global Stewardship, it will be able to provide valuable guidance, and become a powerful agent for change. By reflecting our common values and responsibilities for the present and the future, it will give significant impulses both to research and to action.

The Council will provide an ethical audit on important decisions. It will be a 'community of conscience', with the authority, conferred by the stature of its members, to pronounce on the great issues of our time. It will be legitimized by the quality of its work and its global membership. As a permanent forum, it will act as a global conscience by speaking up for our values, rights and responsibilities as citizens of the world.

It will listen, study and speak out at regular public sessions, nationally and internationally. It will aim to strengthen other initiatives that are seeking to foster global interdependence and responsibility. It will oblige decision-makers to look beyond the political and economic advantages of any given project, and to ask: 'Is it good for people and planet, now or in the future?'

The Council will analyse and quantify the yawning action gaps on important issues such as climate change, deforestation and global inequality, and push for reforms to bridge the gaps between what is currently being done and what actually needs to be done. It will work closely with policy makers, as individuals and through parliamentary groups such as the E-parliament, a new initiative that will electronically link the world's democratically elected MPs. It is envisaged that Council members and MPs will hold joint hearings to formulate and adopt concrete proposals to campaign for in their national parliaments and other relevant bodies.

The Council

The World Future Council will have a core membership of up to 100 persons, consisting of respected individuals from across our planet—wise elders, 'heroes', 'whistle-blowers', 'best practice' pioneers and youth leaders. They will meet annually, addressing key issues of our time. A smaller executive committee will meet more frequently.

The challenge today is not to create 'better' humans but to choose which values our societies should prioritize, respect and protect, for instance:

- Sanctity of life, or commercialization of its building blocks?
- Citizen, or consumer values?
- The well-being of the poor, or the primacy of economics?
- Lifestyles of modest sufficiency, or rampant consumerism?
- Local rights, or global monopolies?
- Reciprocity and solidarity, or competition and profit?
- Human happiness and spiritual well-being, or material growth?
- The interests of future generations, or only our own?
- Mastering, or giving in to our desires?
- Cultural diversity, or global media dominance?

The World Future Council Initiative is now working to develop the WFC, and the practical aspects of this are summarized below. The Initiative has already been endorsed by many leading thinkers and actors across the world, and their names are listed on our website. We will be pleased to add your name and to have a few sentences of support from you.

The Underlying Issues

We have unprecedented power over and responsibilities for both present and future generations. But, blinded by our successes, we have lost our place in the larger story of life as we listen to 'experts' who tell us that society is only a jumble of conflicting interests filled with human "robot vehicles blindly programmed to preserve the selfish molecules known as genes" (Richard Dawkins).

It is claimed that we live in a 'values vacuum', or that people across the world have irreconcilable differences in their value systems. There is little evidence for such claims. Researchers at the Institute for Global Ethics and others have found a remarkable agreement on values and value priorities across continents, faiths, cultures, social classes and religions. This basic consensus overrides diverse world-views and is shared by believers and non-believers of very different backgrounds and countries.

A global citizens' community with common values does not have to be laboriously created. It already exists. But we lack institutions to back up these common values. The key problem is not 'the way we think', but which of our thoughts are respected and acted on by the institutions of power in our societies. We do not face a values gap. We face an action gap.

At a time when the world craves visionary leadership, many of our political leaders have become prisoners of an autistic economic fundamentalism that discounts the future and undermines the values and institutions on which the urgently needed transformation of our societies can be built. They no longer represent us as citizens, but only in our narrow capacity as consumers. They have focused their energies on giving the international legal protection of corporate profits a higher standing than basic human, social and environmental rights. They therefore face cynicism, disinterest and sometimes even violent opposition by all those who feel alienated from a system which offers such dismal choices.

If we want to avoid rising levels of global conflict and environmental stress, we need to re-cast the debate on our future in moral terms, and impose our citizen values on our economics, instead of vice versa. Economic doctrine and its practical policies, i.e. the global capitalist 'growth' model, operate at a fundamental level in contemporary human activities. Its theories have usurped our value systems, cultures and traditions to such an extent that most human, social and environmental problems are now seen as economic. The dominant question is: 'Can we afford it in the short term?'

The orgy of consumerism over the past forty years has not made the global rich any happier. More and more people feel increasingly uncomfortable, fearful and frustrated with a system that sacrifices deeply held values for a single goal—global consumerism—which is in direct conflict with maintaining a liveable planet.

Our leaders deplete our ethical, social and natural capital, 'sell the family silver', monetarize our non-market wealth—and ask to be applauded for this unprecedented 'wealth creation'. They sacrifice the children of the poor on the altar of their accounting practices and banking regulations. They embrace the commodification of life through genetic manipulation, applying a false reductionist and mechanistic mindset to living systems. This economic system is fast becoming humanly, socially and environmentally unaffordable.

In many areas it may already be too late for an orderly transition. Global oil reserves have been exaggerated for political and commercial reasons. Production is expected to peak in a matter of years, severely destabilizing a world order built on cheap oil. The United Nations Environment Programme (UNEP) calculates that climate change could bankrupt the global economy in less than a lifetime unless drastic measures are taken.

We need to de-trivialize the global debate and speak some simple truths. Much of what is currently politically acceptable is in fact international and inter-generational commercial and financial terrorism. His Holiness The Dalai Lama writes in his latest book: "I find it difficult not to suspect that, by means of international debt and the exploitation of natural resources at relatively low cost, the wealth of the rich is maintained through neglect of the poor."

Allowing ever-increasing CO_2 emissions which cause global climate change is a crime against humanity—as are policies forcing the poor to pay dubious debts to the rich while ignoring the historical and ecological debts of the North. Those responsible must be held accountable.

Our ancestors ensured that private corporations, which acted against the common good, could lose their privileges. In the 18th century the British government could dismantle any commercial enterprise "tending to the common grievance, prejudice and inconvenience of His Majesty's subjects". Until quite recently, similar legislation existed in the USA.

The consensus, which permitted such dis-incorporation, was destroyed by a coup d'état of a rich minority—and their servants in politics, the judiciary and the media—who now want to globalize their rules and rule. They claim that we are all united only by common greed. But this is not so. When we are addressed as consumers we respond as such. When nothing else is offered or demanded, shopping becomes the principal cultural expression of 'modern' societies.

Our common values as citizens of the earth are currently drowned out by the cacophony of commercial speech. In our societies the loudest voice is that of advertising. Starting with pre-school children, it aims to foster a culture of permanent dissatisfaction, immaturity and irresponsibility. The youth delegates at the first State of the World Forum (1995) described the consequences: "We currently face a global crisis of the spirit in the search for meaning. As our confidence and self-esteem decline, the value of friendship, family, society, trust and respect begins to lose the battle against selfishness and the pursuit of material gain. It is difficult to know what to believe in these days."

The most serious threat today is not the continuation of present policies—which will soon be impossible. It is the collapse of our societies as our leaders lose their credibility and are replaced by preachers of intolerance and obscurantism in a reaction against market fundamentalism.

New ethical leadership is now needed to counter this global emergency. Twelve years after the Earth Summit in Rio, and two years after the World Summit on Sustainable Development in Johannesburg, the overall signs still point in the wrong direction. There has been a major effort to water-down 'mutual accountability' for dealing with global ills. The debate on shared responsibility is receding and the poor global majority is losing faith in democracy. Even limited agreed reforms, such as the UN Millennium Goals, are unlikely to be implemented in the proposed time horizon.

These are not my conclusions but those of two of the highest-placed insiders in this process, the heads of the World Bank and the United Nations Development Programme, UNDP. We can either fail, and go down in history as accomplices in monstrous crimes, or we can act now.

A Rising Tide of Anger

We are outraged by 'Christian' leaders who insist that the world's poor pay compound interest to the rich even when it costs the lives of their children—in defiance of the command of every religion! We fear for the health of our children, knowing that for many years now mother's milk in many countries is too contaminated to be marketable. We fear the judgment of our grandchildren when the richest nation on earth declares it cannot afford the costs of preventing global climate destabilization, estimated at one per cent of Gross National Product.

We feel hurt to the core of our being by the daily horrors of animal experimentation and of agribusiness: of the 250 million cattle, pigs, horses and sheep transported across Europe every year, many for up to 20 hours without rest or water, 25 million are dead on arrival. We are deeply affected when nature is dying and even the experts admit being 'scared' because no-one knows why—as when large scale fish deaths occurred in the Baltic recently.

We feel diminished by the mechanical dogma foisted upon us, which portrays nature as a mere machine to be manipulated at will. We feel outraged by corporate control over the genetic blueprints of life, and worry about future generations thinking of life as a human invention, with no boundaries between the sacred and the profane. (In the USA, couples can now order a designer child over the internet—eggs, sperm as well as surrogate mothers.)

We feel cheated by the dismissal of deeply held values in the name of economic efficiency; by the promises of a 'micro-millennium' and a 'silicon civilization' of freedom and leisure, against the reality of increasing working hours, and stress or long-term unemployment and exclusion; by the promise of a 'global village' against the reality of a return of the brutal competitive world of the 19th century, in which de-skilling and adversarial money bargaining break down trust and community; by the "ecological aggression of the North against the South" (Klaus Toepfer); by the continued nuclear 'weapons' race, with its potential to poison the earth and its inhabitants for generations to come; by a science that produces toxic cocktails poisoning our water, soil, air and bodies.

I say 'we', because in my experience anger and outrage is a common reaction from those offered the opportunity to respond. It is reflected in reports from all over the world, whether it is 85 per cent in a UK poll demanding the protection of local production from enforced globalization, or the 'citizen juries' in Latin America who overwhelmingly rejected GM foods (after hearing both sides of the argument), and other aspects of corporate-driven globalization.

Many react to the ecological-cultural crisis with despair, searching for scapegoats, becoming addicted or falling ill. The rising tide of intolerance as well as the epidemics of drugs, depression and mental illness in the industrialized countries indicates that we are on a path that is destructive not just to our planet but to our societies and to ourselves.

Economic Totalitarianism

Over 20 years ago, German chancellor Helmut Schmidt found it necessary to justify his country's foreign aid as creating future customers for German exports—a far cry from the poet Hjalmar Gullberg's belief that 'a hungry human being less is a brother/ sister more.' Which reasoning resonates more deeply with us?

Today the whole world is a third world country with a poor majority, and 'the gated communities' of the rich are less and less effective in keeping them out. Either the poor are able to live decently at home or they will come to the rich world in ever increasing numbers. Sending them back will not be a realistic option. In global market societies economic migration is rational, especially when the economic policies imposed on the poor are failing.

Individualistic market ideology teaches that all failure is personal. So instead of staying and fighting injustice at home, many poor people take the rational decision to try elsewhere. Today 85 per cent of young North Africans want to emigrate to the European Union: What will the EU do when the numbers coming increase 10-fold or 100-fold? Trying to keep them out will only increase the number of those who join the most visible global competitor of market fundamentalism: fundamentalist Islam.

All over the world societies that have to educate their children in opposition to the dominant cultural message, i.e. consumerism, are becoming unsustainable: in Thailand, for instance, the Buddhist 'principles of virtuous existence' are no longer being taught beyond primary school. In the USA the sales of anti-depressants to children from the age of two are growing rapidly. In the UK 50 per cent of children under 16 report being 'stressed out', disorientated by the rapid, disruptive changes in a market-driven society.

Today the opposition to the rule of 'economic man'—with its incomplete understanding of human nature—is growing rapidly and it is increasingly values-based. The objections to feeding herbivores such as cows with ground-up dead animals were mainly ethical, as the health risks (BSE) where not yet known. But these objections were rejected as 'unscientific', as are the objections to GM foods today. As a result, 'big science' is increasingly seen with suspicion, as an extension of big business, and no longer to be trusted.

Scientists whose findings disagree with the application of mechanistic thinking to living systems are ignored or dismissed. This was the experience of my biologist grandfather 80 years ago, and of the biochemist Michael Behe (author of *Darwin's Black Box*) in recent years, to mention just two. Consumerism is the 'rational' reaction to this depressing story: if the material is the ultimate reality, then maximizing our material possessions seems a logical way to drown our existential despair. The shopping mall becomes the symbol of a community's modernization.

"Governments should not hinder the logic of the market," says Tony Blair—forgetting that the cornerstones of this market (e.g. limited liability, fractional banking, financial globalization and the WTO), are state-created and dependent on it for their existence. Markets make good servants but bad masters.

By overriding values-based objections in the name of science and economics, we risk "barbarization from within" (Lewis Mumford), for such objections go to the heart of our understanding of what it is to be human. The present global order and economics are based on a materialistic worldview that implies that we are ultimately just products of "accidental collocations of atoms" (Bertrand Russell). This is the modern story we are born into, the 'truth' of a meaningless universe.

Shared Values

We need a new global and inter-generational social contract that reflects our need for balance and sufficiency.
International commissions have shown a remarkable consensus when their members from very different backgrounds and belief systems are asked to focus on the needs of the planet and future generations. It is often claimed that European or Western values prioritize individual rights while Eastern values put communal rights first. But the realities on the ground are different. Over 20 years ago I set up the Right Livelihood Awards, presented annually in the Swedish parliament, with many recipients from other continents. The only times I have ever been accused of not understanding Asian or African values were when the Indonesian and Nigerian dictators complained about awards to human rights activists in their countries.

We all have many different values—we are potentially both devils and angels—but in normal circumstances our value priorities are quite similar. Our ancestors relegated waste and conspicuous consumption to special occasions and feasts—otherwise our planet would probably be uninhabitable by now. Extreme selfishness is usually seen as acceptable only in exceptionally threatening circumstances. People are honoured for what they do for others, for the community. Individualistic greed is frowned upon—except in our modern Western culture, where such behaviour is celebrated as normal and commendable, for it is what the market demands. And as the chairman of the Federal Reserve Board Alan Greenspan said recently: "Markets are the expression of the deepest truth of human nature and will therefore ultimately be correct." But is consumerism really our 'deepest truth'?

The founder of Transpersonal Psychology, Abraham Maslow, pointed out that it is difficult to practice higher values like love, generosity and solidarity in a society whose rules, institutions and information streams are set up to promote lesser human qualities. Most of us are not heroes and will follow the values of power even if we feel uncomfortable doing so. If we are really united only by greed and otherwise divided by deep value differences, then our situation is hopeless. For where is the 'new ethics' and 'new way of thinking', which is increasingly called for, going to come from? What is it to be based on?

But if key human values are shared globally, while the ways we interpret, honour and live them reflect the power relationships in our society, then there is a way forward, because every one of us can contribute to changing existing norms simply by challenging them.

It is sometimes enough just to ask a different question. For instance, we are told that Americans think that the USA pays too much in foreign aid. The 'Americans Talk Issues Foundation' polled Americans on how much aid they thought their country actually pays as a percentage of GDP. Average answer: 18 per cent. What would be fair? Average answer: 5 per cent, i.e. about 50 times more than the US currently pays!

Cutting aid to the poor—and then complaining about economically motivated immigration—is part of the same compartmentalized thinking that worries about increased Chinese consumption, but also about the Japanese not consuming enough. The same mindset wants to lower the retirement age to reduce youth unemployment, but also to raise it to reduce costs. The same mindset worries about the huge level of debt, but worries even more about the consequences if it falls.

A democratic system which keeps us busy choosing between different electricity providers, but does not allow us a choice on issues affecting deeply held values, will not survive. As the Pintasilgo Commission noted a few years ago, "carrying capacity is a function of caring capacity." A political system that fosters greedy individualism is destroying 'caring capacity' at a rate which will soon not just threaten immigrants but the very cohesion of our societies.

Service and Balance

The primary goal of any sustainable human endeavour, including business, must be service and balance, not profit and growth, as our ancestors knew. We need a serious debate about who we are and who we want to be. What sort of relationship with our natural (outer) environment is attuned to our human identity, i.e. our inner environment?

We are the first generation to affect the global climate, and the last that does not have to pay the price for this. The market increasingly crowds out our core survival activities as economically worthless and too time-consuming. It is now well established that the key factors that affect happiness most are mental health, satisfying and secure work, a secure and loving private life, a safe community, freedom and moral values. The political implications of this are devastating, for the current global 'reform agenda' points in the opposite direction—of more insecurity ('mobility', 'flexibility') in return for ever more things. (Its inability to cope with the Japanese, who have decided that they have enough things, illustrates its perversity.)

Increasingly this agenda is facing a 'revolt from the centre'. International youth conferences all over the world have been demanding 'commerce-free space'. In local referenda large majorities, in countries as diverse as Germany and Brazil, reject key aspects of global economic integration. This refusal makes sense in a world of massive unemployment, in which the most secure jobs are actually created by small and medium sized enterprises that produce for regional markets. They create jobs at a fraction of the cost compared with those few created by footloose, global companies that roam the earth like the insatiable 'hungry ghosts' of Buddhism.

It is fashionable today to complain about 'too much government'—while promoting economic globalization which will necessarily mean even more government to protect us from its side-effects. The alternative of more 'regulated self-regulation' must include the right of every community to regulate the extent of its global market integration, e.g. through local content and technology transfer requirements. Such policies have helped countries like the USA, Scandinavia and the Asian 'Tigers' to prosper in the past—but are now outlawed by the World Trade Organisation.

It is increasingly obvious that the ruling ideological paradigm with its mixture of modernist consensus and post-modernist relativism (money rules, science has the truth, everything else is a matter of opinion) is not serving us well. To escape its limitations we need to create the right institutions to guide us on our unprecedented journey, by helping us expand our sense of identity and recognize that we have the knowledge, technology and wealth to create a fair and future-compatible (sustainable) global order in tune with our highest values.

Global Responsibilities and Moral Imperatives

A forum with the ethical and intellectual authority to guide this deep cultural transformation is urgently needed. No other institution is presently filling this gap. The most glaring failure is probably that the majority of religious leaders today lack the courage to speak out against global consumerism and the destruction of biodiversity, and seem to have lost their ability to engage in moral discourse.

The task facing us is huge, but we do not start from zero! The building blocks of a workable global future already exist. Putting them together requires a convincing vision that captivates imagination and inspires action—both of those now excluded, and worried about their family's next meal, and of those who can penetrate and help redirect the global power system towards a just and sustainable order.

The alternatives are becoming clear. Either we are able to respond with the required psychological and spiritual maturity to the unique challenges facing us; or the revolt against market domination of our lives will spread and turn even nastier. History has several examples of mighty materialistic societies collapsing, to be followed by centuries of intolerance, de-skilling, economic collapse, wars and terrorism. But, for the first time, if such a collapse occurs today, it will affect the whole world.

The World Future Council

Speaking for shared human aspirations, values and responsibilities, the Council can become a powerful agent for change. It will help us reclaim our minds and sensitivities, which have been eroded by consumerist brainwashing. It will build on the invaluable work that has already been done by the international community to define our rights and duties as planetary citizens.

The Council will not attempt to 'represent' others, but rather to express and manifest common values and goals—as citizens taking responsibility for the future. It will aim to be a catalytic force that crystallizes the moral & intellectual offensive against the ideology of 'moneytheism'. It will restore confidence in our power to change by inspiring and advancing our vision of possible alternative futures. It will encourage those who feel voiceless, alienated and excluded, and provide leadership and protection for moral courage.

The WFC will help prepare us for the tough decisions ahead by fostering an ethical culture and nurturing mindfulness about the consequences of our actions. It will highlight the ecological, human, social and institutional costs of current 'growth'.

Speaking the language of values, the Council will provide an ongoing reminder of the daily betrayal of future generations. Its standing and moral power will grow as the gap it fills in the architecture of global governance becomes apparent. It will stimulate the creation of national, regional and local Future Councils, and serve as a resource and reference-point for their work. It will ensure that the invaluable work done by international commissions during the past decades is connected, built on and given a permanent voice, instead of being filed away and ignored.

While WFC members will serve in a personal capacity, the aim is to include recognized leaders and representatives of different geographical areas and sectors of society who have shown an awareness and understanding of global values. The Council will be complemented by thematic advisory commissions from civil society, politics, academia, culture, business, etc., dealing with key global issues.

The World Future Council will hold the long-term vision, and ensure that our elected policy makers have access to the best practical visionaries and long-term thinkers when tackling global problems. (The Australian Green Senator, Bob Brown, suggests that above the entrance to every parliament should be the words: 'Will people 100 years from now thank us for what we are doing here?'). The Council could evolve into an elected Earth Senate. Several traditional societies had a 'Council of Seers Into The Future' whose voice was respected when day-to-day decisions were taken.

Creating the WFC

This project is currently co-ordinated by a small international planning committee (IPC). The founding organizations are currently The Right Livelihood Awards Foundation, EarthAction, BAUM (the

Association for Environmental Management), The Global Challenges Network and the UK Schumacher Society.

The WFC Initiative has held preparatory meetings with key thinkers and activists from all continents in Salzburg (Austria) and Tenerife (Spain)—jointly with the e-Parliament Initiative—at the invitation of the regional authorities.

We are aware that at present the WFC Initiative team and office locations are not globally representative. We are working to correct this as a matter of urgency, as our resources permit. This project has been endorsed by many personalities and organizations from the South who wish to help build a fairer global order.

Current WFC Initiative activities include:

- approaching a number of cities and regions, asking them to host all or part of the WFC secretariat, if they can support WFC operations during the 3-5 year initial phase with the help of local sponsors. (Afterwards, the WFC will have become a key part of the global governance structure, able to attract major institutional funding.)

- writing to 8,500 Civil Society Organizations in 170 countries, asking for their support and feedback. They have also been asked to propose names of respected individuals as possible WFC members from their country.

- contacting 15,000 (out of approx. 25,000) democratically-elected national Members of Parliament with the same requests. They will also be asked to indicate on which issues they want to work with the WFC.

- producing several publications, including this book, and the first *World Future Report*, which will summarize the major challenges facing us: where we are now, where we are heading in view of current trends; what practical steps could be taken to meet these challenges.

- building a small Founding Council of respected individuals from among those who have been proposed for WFC membership, to advise and supervise the work of the WFC Initiative.

- exploring, with international legal expertise, the best possible institutional structure for the WFC.

- raising substantial funds to initiate the World Future Council.

WFC Launch and Operations

The WFC will only be launched when the basic funding for its initial phase has been guaranteed. Our aim is not to produce declarations and reports with no process for implementing them. We respect the work being done to develop good reform proposals and do not want to duplicate such work, but to build the framework for a process of implementation.

The initial WFC membership will be selected jointly by the WFC Founding Council and the WFC Initiative from individuals who have received the broadest support during the consultation process, prioritizing those who are respected internationally.

Concerning the legitimacy of this process, it is important to emphasize again that the WFC will ultimately be legitimized by the quality of its work. It will not claim to speak for others and will have no formal powers. All its proposals will have to be approved by democratically-elected policy makers in order to become legally binding. The process of consultation and selection will be the most broad-based and transparent ever held for any such body.

When this process has been completed, the WFC Initiative will hand over control to a WFC board, elected by its membership. This board will commission the WFC Charter, determine the procedures of membership rotation and the selection of new members. Once the WFC is incorporated in the country or countries in which it is headquartered, it will be funded through national foundations, with trustees appointed by the WFC board. The WFC will meet at least annually to hold public hearings and make concrete recommendations, based on the research of its expert commissions.

Implementation

The WFC will be supplemented by advisory commissions on key issues needing global action. Currently we have identified 24 such issues, of which some are very broad and may require smaller subcommissions. There is no need to duplicate existing work. We therefore propose that these commissions be hosted by recognized existing institutions, chosen by the WFC board. The WFC will have its own Research Department to liaise with and co-ordinate their work, to ensure that it fulfils the needs of the Council.

Cities who want to participate in the WFC, but cannot secure the funding required for its secretariats, will also be given the opportunity to host one or more of the commissions. Several institutions and cities have already expressed a strong interest in providing a 'home' for a WFC commission.

The WFC will support global change in a number of ways, through raising the level of public debate and providing a more inter-connected and values-based perspective. But the parliamentary connection is crucial if we are to bridge the current 'implementation gap', when even agreed global initiatives, like the Millennium Development Goals, are not implemented due to institutional blockages.

Reform proposals adopted by the WFC will be presented to MPs who have indicated an interest to work with the WFC in this area. Joint meetings will be held between them and WFC members to develop concrete recommendations (model legislation), to be put to the whole global network of democratic MPs. The e-Parliament

Initiative is developing the facilities for such proposals to be voted on electronically. Proposals with majority support will then be introduced in national parliaments with the help of MPs. The WFC will also work to build worldwide support in national legislatures for the Council's recommendations.

The WFC will encourage the creation of national, regional and local future councils. These will be based on the Swiss model, already adopted in the Canton of Vaud, i.e. have the status of a constitutional body which decision-makers are obliged to take into account. Even without formal 'future veto' powers, the recommendations of such councils would have more weight than purely advisory commissions.

Significant reforms will naturally encounter opposition from vested interests and will not be achieved without substantial civil society support. One of the WFC founding partners, EarthAction, a global network of over 2000 Civil Society Organizations in 170 countries, has a successful track record in mobilizing such support through timely global campaigns and Action Alerts. EarthAction will help initiate and co-ordinate civil society networks on the various themes covered by the WFC commissions, to ensure focused and action-oriented civil society involvement in the WFC process. Through its global network it will engage organizations, citizens and the media to press policy-makers to take action in support of the Council's proposals.

Note: This text aims to stimulate debate about the need for and roles of a World Future Council. The views expressed are those of the author and may not reflect the views of future WFC members. The actual Council may decide to alter the working procedures outlined.

A Call to Action

by Herbert Girardet

The Challenge

To live in a world that is just, peaceful and sustainable is a shared wish of billions of people all over the world. They want to look forward to the future with confidence. But they also know that for decades many global trends have tended to move in the wrong direction, and that, despite many initiatives by the international community, a yawning gap needs to be filled, between where we are and where we want to be.

Modern technology has turned night into day, replaced muscles with motors, and has made us into 'amplified' creatures of enormous power and with vast environmental impacts. It has allowed a small minority of people to acquire unprecedented power, worshipping the here and now as if there were no tomorrow. Never before has a section of society so blatantly ignored the rights and needs of future generations.

Inequality of global income is probably greater today than it has ever been in human history. At present, the richest 1 per cent of people in the world receives as much as the bottom 57 per cent. Even more astonishingly, the 350 richest individuals now have as much wealth as the poorer half of the global population.

We deplore the fact that a few countries claiming to be interested in fostering world peace are still developing ever more sophisticated and expensive weapons of mass destruction. President Eisenhower said on his retirement in 1961: "In the councils of government, we must guard against the acquisition of unwarranted influence, whether sought or unsought, by the military-industrial complex. The potential for the disastrous rise of misplaced power exists and will persist."

The World Future Council (WFC) seeks to be a champion for people concerned with actively creating a just, peaceful and sustainable world. It is all about long-term thinking, and will actively address the historic challenges and systemic problems now facing us. It wishes to reaffirm an ethical consciousness that reflects human rights, as well as human responsibilities.

Planet and People

In recent decades it has dawned on many of us that there can be no viable future for humanity without a healthy planet. Earth, water and air support the existence of an immensely complex living system, powered by the sun. Mountain ranges, rainforests, wetlands, savannahs and coral reefs form the basis for a vast web of life. Humanity is part of this web, and nature's 'ecosystem services' are of tremendous importance to us, and have been valued at tens of trillions of dollars per year.

Humans have always affected the natural environment from which they have drawn their sustenance. Over millennia, the use of fire by our hunter-gatherer ancestors, and the land uses of agricultural societies, have significantly altered the natural world. But the recent emergence of an urban-industrial society has caused unprecedented impacts on the face of the earth.

In the last 100 years in particular, astonishing changes have occurred. Human populations have quadrupled, and resource consumption has increased 16-fold. A small minority, equipped with a vast arsenal of new technologies, has acquired unprecedented power to impose its will on the living earth. Half of us (and rising) have become an industrialized and urbanized species. By drawing on resources from nature, as well as the earth's crust, we dominate our host planet as never before.

Within a few generations we are using up most of the earth's stored resources, particularly fossil fuels. Their transfer from the earth's crust into the atmosphere is significantly altering its composition. From our ever-expanding urban centres, our tentacles now spread across the world. Today our globalizing economic system is destabilizing the planet's life-support systems as well as long-established local economies. Yet we have hardly begun to deal with the crisis now facing humanity:

Environmentally:
- In the 20th century, global forest cover decreased by some 40 per cent

- The greatest loss of species diversity since the last ice age is underway

- Soil erosion now amounts to some 4 tonnes per person/ year

- Climate change is becoming a huge, destabilizing threat

- Glaciers and ice sheets are melting all over the world

- Water shortages are worsening and affecting the lives of billions

- Radioactive releases from nuclear weapons and facilities are a continuing threat

- Millions are becoming refugees due to resource depletion and degraded environments

Socially:
- The richest 20 per cent own 85 per cent of the world's resources

- The poorest 20 per cent own less than 2 per cent

- 2 billion people live in a state of destitution

- 1.3 billion people live in absolute poverty, and 35,000 starve every day

- Billions of city dwellers live under appalling environmental conditions

- Billions of rural people face unacceptable living and working conditions

- A crisis of democracy is spreading across the planet

The World Future Council calls for urgent, systemic changes to establish a sustainable relationship between people and planet. Human activities since the industrial revolution have been essentially *linear*, with ever more resources being taken from nature and toxic wastes being discharged into it. In contrast, natural systems have an essentially *circular metabolism*, in which all wastes become nourishment for future life. For a sustainable world we need to mimic nature's own *circular* system through appropriate use of urban and industrial ecology. It is becoming clear that the ecological redesign of the modern world and its production systems is one of the greatest challenges of the 21st century.

Fortunately, there is a growing awareness that in our victory against nature we may find ourselves on the losing side. Much useful work has already been done, but institutional blockages are delaying action, often due to a lack of clarity about the huge challenges we have to face.

Why a World Future Council?

We have the capacity to build a sustainable future, but we need to bridge both an imagination and an action gap. Despite rapidly growing knowledge of the collision course between the present and the future, companies, nations and the system of international relations, are not making the necessary changes.

At present, even minimal structural changes exceed the maximal implementation capacity of our political and economic systems.

There currently is no international organization engaged in developing a comprehensive overview of all the various dimensions of a just, peaceful and sustainable future. The World Future Council aims to connect up and communicate existing solutions to many of the major issues facing us, and also to ensure that new ones are developed and acted upon.

The last 40 years

Since the 1960s, many people started questioning what is happening to our planet. Wherever they live, they were able to read articles, listen to radio or watch TV programmes about the many urgent issues facing humanity. In amongst escapist programmes, television documentaries and news reports helped to create a new 'global village' consciousness. Many people started to support new NGOs concerned with war and famine, environmental destruction, unsustainable development, global inequalities, racism, unfair trade, lack of women's rights and other urgent issues.

More and more people looked to the United Nations to address the issues, and to deal with the growing crisis in the relationship between people and planet. According to its Charter, the UN has four purposes: to be a centre for harmonizing the actions of nations, to maintain international peace and security, to cooperate in solving international problems, and to promote respect for human rights. During the last 40 years, it has attempted to address many of the urgent issues facing the international community, bringing it together in a series of high level committees and conferences.

A. *Stockholm 1972*

At the Stockholm Environment Summit in 1972 the UN brought the world's governments and civil society together for the first time to discuss the deteriorating relationship between people and planet. At this historic event a catalogue of concerns was first drawn up, making the connection between human rights issues and the growing environmental impacts of an urbanizing and industrializing humanity. For the first time governments from rich and poor countries jointly addressed issues such as pollution control, reforestation, clean development, integrated development planning, conflicts between environment and development, population growth, international cooperation and environmental education.

The Stockholm Declaration was the conference's main outcome. Within its 25 paragraphs the Declaration states: "The natural resources of the earth, including the air, water, land, flora and fauna and especially representative samples of natural ecosystems, must be safeguarded for the benefit of present and future generations through careful planning or management, as appropriate. . . . The capacity of the earth to produce vital renewable resources must be maintained and, wherever practicable, restored or improved. . . . Man has a special responsibility to safeguard and wisely manage the heritage of wildlife and its habitat, which are now gravely imperilled by a combination of adverse factors. Nature conservation, including wildlife, must therefore receive importance in planning for economic development. . . . The non-renewable resources of the earth must be employed in such a way as to guard against the danger of their future exhaustion and to ensure that benefits from such employment are shared by all mankind."

However, the Declaration did not explain how such noble goals were to be achieved.

1972 was also the year in which *Limits to Growth* was published, a book that instantly became an international bestseller. It confirmed people's deepest suspicions about the dangers of unbridled economic growth. For the first time ever, the book attempted to map the future using a specially created computer model called World 3.

Extrapolating from existing trends, it predicted a world running short of resources and suffocating in its own pollution. It sent shockwaves through the worlds of business, commerce and government. Whilst some of its assessments of limits to the availability of key resources were quickly challenged, the book's central idea—that there cannot be unlimited growth in a finite world—has been with us ever since.

In the 1970s, E. F. Schumacher's book *Small is Beautiful* was another significant attempt to rethink a world full of misconceptions regarding the long-term viability of the post-war materialist euphoria. Its great achievement was to challenge some of the basic concepts defining that era: that ever-larger mega-cities, ever-bigger commercial companies, and ever-greater exploitation of the natural world is inevitable. It aimed to redefine economics by suggesting that people and nature mattered above all else. It gave the reader practical and intellectual tools for conceptualizing a new, people-centred, sustainable economy.

Schumacher invented the concept of intermediate technology, aiming to assure its beneficial use for humanity, rather than making humanity a slave to technology. His holistic systems thinking became a source of empowerment to millions of people in many countries. Today Schumacher's legacy lives on in many organizations that bear his name or his intellectual imprint.

But the mega-trends of economic growth and globalization were not easily dislodged. The economic boom, unleashed by privatization from the mid-eighties onwards, heightened concerns about the capacity of the natural world to cope with ever-increasing human demands and impacts. The 'battle for sustainability', waged by environmental groups such as Greenpeace and Friends of the Earth led to a growing public awareness that we were on a collision course with biosphere. Meanwhile the new green parties across Europe began to enjoy growing success, particularly in countries where proportional representation helped them get elected to local and national parliaments.

From the 1980s onwards, several high-level international commissions were set up to investigate the state of the world, and inequalities between rich and poor countries, and to make proposals for change. The Brundtland Commission came up with the concept of sustainable development, defining it as 'development that meets the needs of the present without compromising the ability of future generations to meet their own needs'. The Commission wanted to find ways to improve the living conditions of billions of poor people whilst also reducing human environmental impacts.

B. Rio and its legacy

Sustainable development became the basic concept for the negotiations between UN member states at the 1992 Rio Earth Summit. World leaders, spurred on by civil society, set out to initiate a wide range of measures to address the growing environmental and social emergency across the planet. International agreements on economic and social development, deforestation, climate change and biodiversity were drawn up. Rio seemed to be a significant turning point, "a transformation of our attitudes and behaviour", according to the UN. Most importantly, it gave rise to Agenda 21, defining practical steps that governments, businesses, local authorities and citizens could take towards creating a sustainable world.

But a few powerful countries showed that the constraints on business as usual imposed by sustainable development were not to their liking. Under President George Bush Senior, the US delegation, in particular, effectively sabotaged the proposed climate change treaty, gutted and then refused to sign the biodiversity convention, and replaced an internationally binding forest protocol with a set of weak and voluntary 'forest principles'.

Since Rio, even the very limited commitments agreed by the world's governments have been largely broken. Their record on moving towards environmental sustainability has been very poor indeed, particularly in two crucial areas: the onslaught on rainforests has been allowed to continue apace, and the increase of CO_2 in the atmosphere has accelerated rather than slowed down. Meanwhile a large proportion of humanity still lack access to enough food, clean water, adequate sanitation, electricity and other essentials of modern life.

However, the good news is that throughout the 1990s, under the auspices of Agenda 21, millions of people have worked hard towards implementing sustainable development at local and regional levels, often supported by national legislation and regulation. There have been some significant successes, and journalists and environmental campaigners have widely documented and publicized these.

But sadly, many of the trends first discerned in the mid-seventies are coming home to roost. 1.2 billion people in the world who go to bed hungry are now matched by the same number suffering from obesity. Climate change is now upon us with a vengeance. Some 24 billion tonnes of soil per year are eroding due to unsustainable farming methods, as forests are cleared and marginal land is taken over for farming. An urbanizing and industrializing humanity is also eroding its inherited understanding of the vital functions of nature in our lives. These developments make it ever harder to find solutions for some problems facing us.

C. Urbanization and the 1996 UN City Summit

In the last 100 years an extraordinary change started to occur across the planet: urbanization has accelerated as never before. Cities are becoming humanity's primary habitat: from living in a world of farms, villages and small towns, we are transforming ourselves into an urban species. From drawing on local energy sources, we have switched to tapping into stores of non-renewable energy resources across the world. From leading locally self-sufficient lives, more and more of us are becoming citizens of an interconnected human-centred planet.

In 1900, 15 per cent of a global population of 1.5 billion people lived in cities. By 2000, 47 per cent of a global population of 6 billion had become urbanized. In 1900, four cities of around one million— Beijing, Tokyo, Delhi and London—were the largest cities on earth. By 2000 there were 200 cities of one million, 100 between one and ten million, and some 20 megacities of more than ten million people. By 2030, 60 per cent of the world population, or 4.9 billion people, are expected to live in urban areas.

In 1996 the UN called its second City Summit, recognizing that sustainable urbanization is a major new challenge for humanity. Megacities of ten million people or more are by far the largest structures and the most complex manifestation of human activity ever to emerge. They reach deep underground, rise high into the air, and stretch out over several hundred thousand hectares, with fossil fuel powered transport routes linking them to each other and to a global hinterland.

To make current urban lifestyles possible, cities are sucking in resources from all over the world. Located on just two per cent of the world's land surface, they use 75 per cent of its resources. If the energy use of urban food supply systems was included, this figure would be even higher. In the USA the number of people fed per farm worker has grown more than six fold, from 15 in 1950 to 96 in 1998, by a massive scaling up of the use of farming technology. In an urbanizing world, the combined *ecological footprints* of cities extend to much of the earth's productive land.

The role of cities in reducing these impacts is now widely acknowledged. In Istanbul, the Habitat Agenda was endorsed by 180

.nations. It states: 'Human settlements shall be planned, developed and improved in a manner that takes full account of sustainable development principles and all their components, as set out in Agenda 21.... We need to respect the carrying capacity of ecosystems and preservation of opportunities for future generations. Production, consumption and transport should be managed in ways that protect and conserve the stock of resources while drawing upon them. Science and technology have a crucial role in shaping sustainable human settlements and sustaining the ecosystems they depend upon'.

Cities all over the world have started to implement significant initiatives on sustainable development, but the total impact of urban consumption and waste disposal on nature is still increasing. Much needs to be done to wean cities off their dependence on fossil fuels, and to create sustainable, solar cities.

D. The other UN summits

In addition to the Earth Summits and the City Summit, the UN also held a series of other global conferences: on Nuclear Disarmament, Population Growth, Human Rights, Women's Rights, the Rights of the Child, Racism, AIDS, as well as the ongoing highly controversial negotiations of the WTO on expanding world trade.

Climate change has been the subject of a series of high-level international meetings, starting with the Kyoto conference in 1997. Agreement in principle was reached to reduce global greenhouse gas emissions by 60 per cent by 2050. But by 2004 the required number of countries—representing 55 per cent of total CO_2 discharged into the atmosphere—had still not signed up, and therefore the Kyoto Treaty has still not been formally implemented. It is also becoming increasingly apparent that Kyoto itself is only a faltering first step in the right direction. Far more radical targets will need to be implemented to prevent a world-wide climate disaster. The London-based

Global Commons Institute has proposed a global process of Contraction and Convergence, with equal per-capita allowances for greenhouse gas emissions for all the world's countries. This has gathered much international support, but implementation is being blocked by those with a powerful interest in the status quo.

There is no doubt that the world has benefited from the fact that many high-level international conferences have been held and many new international links have been established in recent years. In particular, thousands of NGOs have prodded the world's governments to get serious about bridging the *action gap*—the gap between the status quo and what needs to be done to create a just and sustainable world.

All the major UN conferences have ended in elaborate declarations: they reflect the noble aims of large sections of the international community, but also the lowest common denominator compromises that bedevil international negotiations. The legacy of recent UN conferences is a crucial lack of co-ordinated implementation plans and of binding commitment of resources. In the coming years we need to assure that we won't again be let down by those global players who claim that they know how to tackle the huge challenges we face, yet do little to address them.

E. UN Millennium Goals

The urgent need to set new agendas is well illustrated by the story of the UN's Millennium Goals. In September 2000 the United Nations held a special General Assembly which indicated a significant new trend: that the global community is showing concern about the condition of large sections of humanity, but that the environmental condition of the planet is slipping down the priority list. The Assembly published a set of millennium goals, to be reached by 2015. They include the aims to:

- Halve infant mortality rates in Sub-Saharan Africa

- Halve the proportion of people living on less than one dollar a day

- Halve the number of people without access to safe drinking water

- Halt and begin to reverse the spread of HIV/AIDS

- Halt and begin to reverse the incidence of malaria and other major diseases

- Achieve significant improvement in the lives of at least 100 million slum dwellers

- Develop further a rule-based, open trading and financial system

- Provide universal access to primary education

- Integrate sustainable development into country policies and programmes, and

- Reverse loss of environmental resources.

But even these mainly socially focussed goals—which largely ignore the imperative of an environmentally healthy planet—are highly unlikely to be achieved by 2015. The unwillingness of the richer countries, in particular, to address these vital issues is ever more evident.

UNDP director-general Mark Malloch Brown said recently: "The solutions are known. What is lacking is the political will to implement them . . . The emerging countries are improving their living standards. But the poorest countries have seen their human development indexes shrink as never before. At the current pace, in sub-Saharan Africa the UN development goals will be achieved only in 2147."

World Bank president James Wolfensohn stated at another conference: "Every year the most powerful nations of the world spend over 1,000 billion dollars in weapons, 350 billion dollars in subsidies for agriculture, but only 57 billion dollars in development aid."

F. The Johannesburg Summit

The UN Millennium Assembly also decided to call a third Earth Summit in 2002, to be held in Johannesburg and to be called the World Summit on Sustainable Development. At the time, UNEP director general Klaus Toepfer stated: "When the United Nations General Assembly authorized holding the World Summit on Sustainable Development, it was hardly a secret . . . that progress in implementing sustainable development has been extremely disappointing since the 1992 Earth Summit, with poverty deepening and environmental degradation worsening. What the world wanted, the General Assembly said, was not a new philosophical or political debate but rather, a summit of actions and results."

The 2002 Johannesburg Summit was called to review outcomes of the Rio Summit and, if possible, to accelerate action. But after two weeks of negotiations it became apparent that many of the world's governments were not prepared to subscribe to significant new measures and to make the required financial commitments.

The Summit was the first—and largely missed—opportunity of the 21st century to transcend what politicians regard as *possible* by implementing what is *necessary*. But few governments there were infused with a sense of urgency and a spirit of creativity. Blandness, indecision and negativity prevailed. The Summit's very limited achievement was a further refinement of the UN millennium goals concerned primarily with improving the living conditions for underprivileged people in the world's ever growing cities. The conference's main outcome, the 'Johannesburg Plan of Implementation', contains non-binding targets and timetables on a small range of issues, such as:

- Halving the proportion of people who lack access to clean water or proper sanitation by 2015

- Restoring depleted fisheries by 2015

- Reducing biodiversity loss by 2010, and

- Using and producing chemicals in ways that do not harm human health and the environment by 2020.

During the summit, news broke that the planet's glaciers and ice shelves are melting faster than ever. But George W. Bush's administration scuppered plans by the European countries for setting targets for the large-scale introduction of renewable energy across the world. Because of the position taken by the USA and a few other countries, the Summit made no statements on climate change at all, and could only agree to increase the use of renewable energy "with a sense of urgency".

Nevertheless, United Nations Secretary-General Kofi Annan stated at a closing press conference in Johannesburg. "This Summit makes sustainable development a reality. This Summit will put us on a path that reduces poverty while protecting the environment, a path that works for all peoples, rich and poor, today and tomorrow."

Few people present at the summit could share the optimism of this statement. The fact is that the mega-trend of economic globalization, driven by some transnational corporations, is continuing to widen global inequalities: one-tenth of humanity now consumes some 70 per cent of the world's resources. Human 'full spectrum dominance' over nature is continuing to increase: today one single species, out of tens of millions of species, claims half of nature's annual production for itself, as well as all the world's mineral resources. Species are disappearing or being depleted at an unprecedented pace.

The pillage of both mineral resources and living nature is better documented than ever before. WWF's *Living Planet Report 2002*, published just before the Summit, indicates that that over a third of the natural world has been lost in the last 30 years through processes such as rainforest destruction, expansion of farmland, desertification and damage to coral reefs. Human demand already exceeds nature's supply and our global ecological footprints now exceed the earth's sustainable carrying capacity by some 20 per cent. We are eating into the earth's natural capital and are outrunning the capacity of the biosphere to regenerate. If the whole world were to adopt the consumption patterns of the developed countries, three planets would be required rather than the one we actually have to live on. Yet in Johannesburg these realities were all but ignored by governments.

The conference witnessed a deep divide between the NGOs, who wanted binding targets on global sustainability, and many governments and corporations, who wanted to preserve a convenient status quo of voluntary agreements. The result is that the global action gap has opened up further than ever before, despite the fact that we have ever greater problems to deal with.

G. The UN Commission on Sustainable Development

Following on from the UN's major conferences in recent years, several new UN commissions were created—on global governance, on protecting the global commons, on climate change and on poverty alleviation. Perhaps most notable is the UN Commission on Sustainable Development, the CSD. Its twelfth session met at the UN Headquarters in New York in April 2004.

The CSD functions on the basis of two-year 'Implementation Cycles'—with each cycle focussing on a cluster of issues. In the first year of each cycle it evaluates progress made in implementing sustainable development commitments made in Agenda 21, the Johannesburg Plan of Implementation, and relevant CSD sessions, and the focus is on identifying obstacles and constraints. In the second the CSD decides on measures to speed up implementation, and mobilize action to overcome obstacles and constraints, and to build on the lessons that have been learned.

As with every cycle in the new work programme, the 2004 meeting aimed to tackled a number of cross-cutting issues, such as:

- Poverty eradication

- Unsustainable patterns of production and consumption

- Protection of the natural resource base of economic & social development

- Sustainable development in a globalizing world

- Health and sustainable development

- Sustainable development for Africa and other regions

- Institutional frameworks for sustainable development

But little concrete action has so far emerged from these high-level discussions.

H. The Global Environment Facility

The Global Environment Facility (GEF), established in 1991, has 176 member countries, and funds projects and programmes that protect the global environment. It works in the developing world, Eastern Europe, and the Russian Federation—more than 140 countries altogether. GEF grants support projects focus on biodiversity, climate change, international waters, land degradation, the ozone layer, and persistent organic pollutants. The GEF has been particularly active in supporting renewable energy programmes. Its implementing agencies—UNDP, UNEP and the World Bank—manage GEF projects on the ground. GEF funds are contributed by donor countries and since 1991, the GEF has provided $4.5 billion in grants and generated $14.5 billion in co-financing from other partners. In 2002, 32 donor countries pledged $3 billion to fund operations between 2002 and 2006.

These are significant initiatives, which ought to be respected. There are, of course, many other initiatives and partnerships around the world concerned with implementing sustainable development initiatives. However, to get to grips with the huge challenges facing humanity, far greater sums need to be made available to implement sustainable development than have, so far, been pledged by the world community. For instance, far organizations such as the World Bank still invest far more money fossil fuel technology than on renewable energy. All too often money is spent on trying to fix problems after they have occurred, rather than preventing their occurrence in the first place.

Needed: a New Development Model

The Johannesburg Summit confirmed a deep suspicion held by many people, that we are faced with a profound failure of world governance. The fact is that today an acute State of Emergency exists on earth, imperilling its climate, its life support systems and the lives of billions of people. The single-minded quest for economic success by small sections of humanity, based on the unprecedented use of technology and throughput of resources, is leading to environmental catastrophe and threatens the life support systems of billions of people. The related crises of unprecedented environmental degradation across the world and the destitution of a third of humanity need to be addressed is a new, systemic and imaginative way.

The current trends are vividly illustrated by the growing concerns of the insurance industry. In December 2003 Munich Reinsurance, the world's biggest reinsurance company, expressed alarm about a sharp increase in climate-related disasters. Some 20,000 people were killed by that year's summer heat wave in Europe, which is widely attributed to global warming. On present trends, economic losses from environmental stress could exceed the total value of human production in just two generations.

It is becoming apparent not only that more needs to be done but that different strategies are needed to bridge a growing action gap.

The WFC's unique structure and process, working with both MPs and NGOs, will help to push for the implementation of urgent reforms. It will challenge the claims of the global players who assured the world in Rio and Johannesburg that they were best equipped to tackle the world's problems.

The world community is called to act according to a planetary ethic—of respect for life and human dignity. This ethic is eloquently expressed in documents such as the Earth Charter, and it is crucial to build on such existing initiatives. But, above all else, the unprecedented crisis we are now facing also requires vigorous action.

We may consider ourselves as a VIP species, but we will not get away with breaking the ground rules of living together as a vast web of life on earth. Billions of people worldwide are becoming aware of the connectedness of all life. As the world wakes up from complacency and 'numbed out' isolation from one another, it is starting to recognize our common humanity and the challenges we need to face together.

At this defining moment in history, there is overwhelming evidence that we need to give priority to major investment in environmental security, justice and peace, not war. Jointly, we can work to:

- create a participative Earth Democracy—fundamentally reforming global governance, assuring that international decision making is open and accountable

- assure action and sufficient funds to protect and restore the earth's damaged ecosystems

- rapidly phase in renewable energy technology in place of polluting energy systems

- develop and promote strategies for sustainability in industry and transport

- create ecological economies, compatible with the earth's ecosystems—acknowledging that perpetual economic growth is not possible in a finite world

- revive local democracies and economies—prioritizing local production for local consumption, and minimizing the need for long-distance transport of goods

- make sustainable agriculture the global norm—securing food supplies with minimal environmental impacts

- create liveable and sustainable human settlements across the world

- shift taxation from labour to the use of resources, pollution and waste—promoting conservation and clean production, and enhancing social welfare and jobs

- reform monetary and financial systems to protect and enhance the well-being of human communities and the natural environment on which they depend

- help initiate a progressive shift of funds from military spending towards environmental security—providing adequate water, nutrition, healthcare, shelter and sustainable livelihoods for all

- protect tribal and traditional societies and their lands —acknowledging their right to decide their own future and respecting their contribution to human knowledge

World Future Council: Influence and Effectiveness

The World Future Council Initiative calls for a new, global alliance of members of all sections of society. It wishes to emphasize the importance of cultural creativity in solving the many serious problems facing us. The creative energy of all of humanity is needed—

using traditional and popular knowledge, art, design, engineering, modern science and business—to create a thriving and sustainable relationship between people and planet.

In addition to the World Future Council itself, we also call for the development of national, regional and local Future Councils, closely linked to MPs and NGOs. Today we have a new network that can help to bind humanity together: the internet. By working together through our local and global networks, we can accelerate initiatives already under way, shifting the global balance of power in favour of restoring the earth, sharing its resources equitably, and assuring the sustainable well-being of present and future generations.

We need a globally equitable system for harvesting the earth's resources agreed upon by humanity. A couple of decades of unrestrained, market-driven economic expansionism has been a disaster for the global environment and many of the world's people. Markets themselves are not sufficient as regulatory mechanisms. Above all else, they encourage efficiency, but not equality or, indeed, sustainability.

We need to better understand the complex relationships between economic, social and environmental issues. The 'global village' means international cooperation for achieving sustainable economies, which assure that local consumption is met by local production wherever possible. Trade could be increasingly dematerialized, with ideas rather than products being exchanged worldwide wherever possible.

Bridging the Action Gaps

A key focus for WFC's work, then, is to identify and quantify the 'action gaps' between the status quo and a just, peaceful and sustainable world. In recent years the global citizen's movement has clearly defined many of the measures that need to be taken, and we can build on the rich variety of ideas that have emerged. This is a historic moment for linking acute awareness of problems with implementation of practical, long-term solutions to build a new, global agenda of sustainability, peace and justice.

At the start of the 21st century we are seeing a new world in the making—'another world is possible', and it is beginning to take shape. Human experience accumulated over tens of thousands of years must contribute to a sustainable future, as unprecedented numbers of people from so many different cultures live on this planet together. The World Future Council will affirm our common values and the unacceptability of stealing from future generations. As the voice of the earth, of the future, and of global sanity, it will show effective ways forward and help to restore public trust in global governance.

The Commissions

The World Future Council will set up 24 small expert Commissions to cover some of the major challenges facing humanity. These Commissions, with participants selected after wide consultation, will begin their work as soon as resources are available. They will delegate members to the annual meeting of the WFC to define and publicize its proposals for action. The following is a provisional list of the commissions and the issues they are likely to deal with:

A. Environment

1. Healthy Food for All

UN figures show that global food supplies are more than adequate, producing 1.5 times the amount required to feed the world. But desertification and soil erosion are rapidly decreasing the available arable land. Alternative food production systems need greater credence: Cuba now produces more food than before with greatly reduced chemical inputs. Permaculture cultivation produces more energy than it consumes, and is operational in many countries. Domestication of edible wild perennials can increase per-acre yields and may herald a new agricultural revolution.

Why are we allowing 35,000 people to die of starvation every day, and how can the human right to nourishing food be implemented? Is a reduction of global meat production necessary and possible? Is pesticide poisoning of some 25 million people a year acceptable? Can organic farming feed the world? What are the pros and cons of subsidized large-scale agribusiness? What are the best ways to reform it? Can we develop a new social contract between society and agriculture, assuring sustainable yields and healthy food from efficiently farmed land?

2. Clean Water for All

Global water availability is limited. Water is being wasted by the rich, becoming unaffordable for the poor and polluted by both. Privatization is being promoted as the best way of making adequate supplies of safe water available in poor countries. Despite growing concerns about their environmental and social impacts, large dams are still being constructed to 'assure' water supplies in places where efficient water systems could be employed with minimal impacts.

What are the political, educational and technical changes needed to ensure sufficient clean water for all? How quickly can a global clean water programme be implemented and who will pay? In areas of extreme water shortages, how can these best be dealt with? How can urban wastewater be used in food production? Which technical solutions work best and in which circumstances? How can sustainable water supplies for future generations be safeguarded?

3. Safe Energy and Transport

There is little doubt about the seriousness of the global energy crisis. Our current energy system uses up scarce fossil fuels a million times faster than nature produces them. Cheap fossil fuel energy is a key ingredient in modern cities and their transport systems. If the era of cheap oil and gas ends before a viable alternative energy order is in place, the widespread disruption of our societies is threatened. Few people regard nuclear energy, which leaves wastes that remain highly toxic for geological time periods, as a plausible alternative.

What incentives are needed to affect a timely implementation of energy efficiency and a rapid changeover to renewables? How can institutional blockages to renewable energy be overcome and 'best-practice' policy be transferred across countries? How can we ensure that 'clean' energy development does not mean delayed development? Can we reduce our reliance on global transport systems? How can we close down nuclear power stations safely? Can oil producers be persuaded to keep oil in the ground for sustainable use by future generations?

4. Tackling Climate Change

There is now little doubt that climate change has become a reality. Glaciers are melting all over the world. Weather patterns are becoming more erratic. The IPPC forecasts increases of global mean temperatures of up to 5.8 degrees this century and sea level rises of up to one metre. Half the world's people live within 50 km of seashores, and their lives will be severely affected by flooding. Up to a million species of plants and animals could be lost due to climate change.

Are viable transitional scenarios available to deal with climate change? Can the widely acclaimed Contraction and Convergence scenario be implemented through international agreement? Can emissions trading be made to work and what are its limits? Could biological and technical carbon sequestration be part of a transitional strategy over the coming decades? Is adaptation to rather than prevention of climate change a realistic scenario?

5. Sustainable and Liveable Cities

At present cities, on two per cent of the earth's surface, cities use 75 per cent of its resources. In the 'age of the city' we need new parameters for urban planning. The sustainable, resource efficient city is one of the great challenges of the 21st century. Much also needs to be done to deal with the inhospitality of modern cities. Concrete measures must be taken to reduce the need for travel, revive public transport and to reduce the dependence on the private motorcar.

What policy measures are needed to improve the resource productivity of our cities? How can we create cities that have a 'circular metabolism', that function well on a frugal use of resources, and whose wastes do not overload nature? How can we create attractive public spaces, buildings and markets? How can we assure a greater presence of nature in the urban fabric? How can cities more effectively learn from one another about sustainability and liveability?

6. Intelligent and Sensitive Building

Our ancestors often created houses that were beautiful, regionally adapted and built to last—despite their 'poverty'. They also created magnificent buildings of worship and public structures that have withstood the test of time. In contrast, modern architects have often been forced to construct soulless, poorly insulated mass housing. The poorest are given the most inadequate buildings to live in. Many modern buildings will last no more than a generation.

How can best practice in architecture become normal practice? How can we create new frameworks for building affordable, healthy, beautiful and energy efficient housing? Shouldn't the poor have an equal right to good and beautiful housing? Does the public have a right to influence what buildings go up in the environment around them? How can we assure that citizens become actively involved in shaping the built environment in their neighbourhoods?

7. Sustainable Use of Forests

The rich countries have decimated their forests long ago and yet they are telling poor countries not to do the same. Timber demands by rich countries mean unprecedented forest destruction and an associated loss of biodiversity in the tropics, whilst ancient forests in countries like Russia are also being decimated. We are mining virgin forests without adequately understanding the consequences, and we often replace them with monocultures that are highly unsustainable.

What needs to be done to assure a wider understanding of the value of forest biodiversity? How can we assure sustainable global timber supplies? How far can tree plantations take the pressure off virgin forest? Can we curtail our demand for timber and paper to reduce pressure on forests? Can forests play a role in carbon sequestration in an age of climate change?

8. Sustainable Use of the Oceans

Until recently the oceans seemed too large to be polluted or overfished, and there has been little understanding of the sustainable limits of their use. But recently both sea pollution and a deepening crisis of fish stocks have become a global concern. Coral reefs, 'the rainforests of the sea', are nurseries for a vast variety of species. Today they are under unprecedented pressure from pollution, mining and global warming. We need far better understanding of what measures are required to protect the oceans as global commons and to enhance sustainable practices.

Can global agreements for ocean protection be agreed and implemented? How can individual countries learn from best practice in sustainable fishing? How can oil spills, pollution and harmful emissions from shipping be minimized? Can global measures to protect coral reefs be made to work? Can fish farms compensate for loss of fish stocks in the oceans? Can the ecological and health problems associated with fish and prawn farming be overcome?

B. Economics and Politics

9. Good Work for All

Much work being done by people today is destructive to the planet, carries unnecessary risks to workers, is boring and does not pay a living wage. Local economies everywhere are threatened by economic globalization, and yet jobs for local markets can often be created at a fraction of the cost of jobs for global markets. In the 'developed countries', many skilled workers are unemployed whilst 'developing countries' often suffer from severe skills shortages.

What can we do to assure a better global division of labour? How can working conditions and job opportunities be created that benefit both people and planet? What reforms are required to create a better and more sustainable work situation, actively involving workers and benefiting consumers? How should work be remunerated to maximize the creation of true wealth?

10. Responsible Entrepreneurship

On a finite planet there cannot be an infinite growth of economic activity. There is much evidence of the need to refocus the entrepreneurial spirit on the primacy of service and responsibility, for both people and planet. There may be a case for disbanding corporations that are putting profits before social benefit, and that doing more harm than good environmentally.

Where can the profit motive help and where does it harm? What can be done to assure that maximum rather than reasonable profits become a primary focus of business? What are the best ownership models for large enterprises? Should parts of society be commerce-free and based on social entrepreneurship? How can the duties of economic globalization become transparent and enforceable? What are the limits and consequences of personal responsibility?

11. Monetary and Tax Reforms

Financial wealth has exploded far beyond the growth of real wealth—yet we are told that there is not enough money for urgently needed reforms. We tax human labour until it is often unafford-able—yet subsidize and discount the use of scarce resources. We need to understand much better how money is created. There is an urgent need to regulate the financial system to meet the needs of people and to respect natural limits.

How is real wealth best measured? What role can local and regional currencies play? How can urgent reforms be funded? Is it acceptable for governments to reduce their sovereign right to issue money in favour of debt-based money created by private banks? What are the pros and cons of a banking system based on interest? Is the Islamic financial system a viable alternative? Is the Jubilee Year concept of periodic debt forgiveness of highly indebted countries enforceable? What kind of tax reforms can assure the efficient and clean use of resources?

12. Opportunities and Limits of Trade

Humanity has always been involved in trade and exchange, and has greatly benefited from this. But today trade is often destructive and harmful. It is time to define the main areas of damaging and unsustainable trade and how these could be controlled. The key environmental and social externalities should be internalized to ensure full cost accounting of the impacts of trading.

What is the optimum balance between self-reliance and global market integration? What are the pros and cons of fostering export dependency as the prime route of development? Could a new fair trade regime provide a better deal for poor countries? How can the WTO's powers be balanced internally and externally to ensure that its trade promotion agenda does not harm more important human goals, and does not damage the global environment?

13. Zero Waste Production

The industrialization of the world based on the current model is ecologically impossible. Already the industrial countries face very substantial legacies of toxic residues in their soil and water that are extremely costly to remove. Poor countries will follow the current path until a better one is in sight. The parameters of clean industrialization need to be much better defined. New incentives are needed to spread eco-industrial design, based on bio-degradable product lifecycles.

How can we assure the widespread adoption of zero waste production systems? What tests should be required before new products are permitted? How can non-toxic alternatives be promoted and accelerated? How can we assure sustainable global industrialization? What are the parameters of such a system and how do we reach international agreements on these? Can the leasing principle be made mandatory to encourage product redesign from the bottom up?

14. Reform of International Institutions

After World War Two, the pre-war international system was largely replaced by one adapted to the new world order. It is unclear whether this system can still usefully serve today's very different world. There have been many proposals for UN reform, all blocked by lack of political will and sectoral interests. We need a global discussion on which international institutions have outlived their usefulness, which ones need reforms, and what new institutions are needed.

What can be learnt from the failures of global governance? Which are the urgent proposals for change for which a broad coalition could be mobilized? How can a sensible hierarchy of appropriate international agreements be implemented? How can the global majority cooperate better when faced with the growing obstruction of powerful countries? How can the global majority—and the interests of future generations— influence the decision-making of international institutions? Should the proposals by Keynes for a fairer trade and financial order be revived?

15. Nuclear Disarmament

The threat of nuclear war may appear less than at the height of the Cold War but the dangers remain huge. The major nuclear powers still point thousands of missiles at each other, each one capable of inflicting unimaginable suffering on millions of uninvolved people and future generations. The refusal of the major powers—especially the USA—to accept nuclear disarmament has encouraged nuclear proliferation in areas of conflict. Israel, for instance, is reliably estimated to have over 200 nuclear warheads.

What can be done to challenge the insistence of the United States to claim the right to use nuclear weapons first at a time when it has no enemy with superior conventional forces? How can a global campaign to enforce The Hague Court's ruling on nuclear weapons be sustained? What can non-nuclear states do together to keep this issue in the public and political arena?

16. Biological, Chemical and Conventional Disarmament

Creating a world free from weapons is another great challenges of the 21st century. The current threats of terrorism and the daily carnage from small arms, mines and bombs highlights the need for a permanent forum to investigate and lobby in these areas. A number of NGO and intergovernmental initiatives are working to mobilize public opinion and they could benefit from the higher profile that the hearings of the World Future Council would ensure.

What can be done to highlight the implementation deficit of existing conventional arms agreements? How can we expose the hypocrisy of the continuing arms trade by major countries? What steps need to be taken at all levels—from the personal to the global—to bring about major changes in public opinion and vigorous initiatives towards disarming the world?

C. Social Issues

17. Human Rights and Responsibilities

Rights remain empty unless there is a responsibility to secure them. Proclaiming unenforceable rights may have a moral relevance but can breed cynicism. The Declaration of Human Rights and the UN Charters and Conventions have built a body of international soft law, complemented by the hard law of The Hague Court judgments and agreements containing sanctions. But implementation remains patchy and unbalanced.

The Declaration of Human Duties and Responsibilities, prepared for UNESCO in 1998 but never brought to a vote, provides a starting point for a world order where human rights are secured by corresponding moral duties and legal responsibilities of various actors and levels of society. How can it be implemented? How can human rights best be enforced? Is the concept of interconnected human rights and responsibilities useful?

18. Revitalizing Democracy

Our democratic systems of governance are facing a growing crisis of confidence. Fewer people vote and a smaller part of each voter votes:

we are addressed only as 'political consumers' and thus vote only our consumer preferences. Our deeper citizen priorities and values are ignored in sound-bite election campaigns that offer few alternatives. As a result governments and political parties are trusted less and less and voters are becoming disillusioned. This development holds the risk that in a crisis situation, 'strong men' offering scapegoats could have mass appeal.

How can we rehabilitate democracy—from the local to the global level? Should local direct democracy be reintroduced, with the right to vote directly, e.g. on spending priorities, as the PT has done in Brazil? How can we democratize global decision-making? Would an electronic Earth Parliament ('E-Parliament'), where all democratically elected MPs have the right to introduce and vote for model legislation, be workable and effective?

19. Peace Education and Conflict Healing
In a crowded and individualistic world, peaceful living together is not easy. We have lost the basic trust and connectedness in faith which our ancestors felt, and we often feel threatened by change we don't understand. Conflicts between people are easy to start and hard to heal. Many techniques have been developed to stop conflicts from turning violent, yet few people are aware of these. Best practices should be highlighted yet don't get adequate attention in the media.

Which electoral system strikes the best balance between minority and majority rights—and obligations? How can peaceful co-existence best be taught? How can the media be used in conflict healing? At what stage of a peace process are causes of conflict best focused upon? What are the optimum times and methods for outside intervention? What role should truth commissions play in conflict resolution?

20. Health and Medicine

Despite the huge achievements of modern sanitation and medicine, humanity faces vast and costly health challenges. New epidemics, environmental illnesses and sensitivities, side effects of drugs and unhealthy lifestyles are affecting the lives of billions. Present health education systems are inadequate for making people sufficiently aware of the variety of health threats. The potential for popular participation of a well-informed public in health care is greatly underrated.

What are the priorities for medical, economic and political reform to optimize health? How can medical training be reformed so that patients are treated as living beings, rather than collections of symptoms? How can different schools of diagnosis and healing be better integrated to help patients choose appropriate methods of healing? How can our right to be protected from potentially toxic new chemicals be ensured in an economically globalized world?

21. Education and the Media

Our educational system is struggling to maintain its relevance in a fast-changing world. Learning never stops, and people need to continuously enhance their knowledge. Global communications has taken on a quasi-educational role, yet mass entertainment should not be confused with the spread of knowledge. A global consumerist monoculture can only be countered by safeguarding the individual right to choose lifestyles within sustainable limits. We need to find new ways of safeguarding the values of a free media whilst enforcing the responsibilities of the media.

How can our educational systems be adapted and enabled to provide appropriate tuition for all at all ages? How can 'commerce-free education' be safeguarded? What is the role of the state in supporting and promot-

ing education and culture? In an ever-faster age, how can we protect slow learners? What best practices exist to overcome the digital divide? How can computer literacy be spread without further supporting the global monopoly of a few corporations?

22. Indigenous People and Bio-cultural Diversity
In the eyes of many, indigenous people are the 'keepers of the whole', holding on to ancient wisdom that can serve as a valuable guide in these confused times. Their cultures need to be protected and their knowledge preserved while respecting their desire to choose different lifestyles. Better ways need to be found to safeguard their rights to often sparsely populated areas against the pressures of their neighbours.

What legal reforms are needed to safeguard the rights of indigenous communities to public goods and the global commons? Are there countervailing indigenous responsibilities, e.g. for land use and preservation and the sharing of knowledge? Can shared community values be protected against individual consumer values? How can indigenous wisdom help global society to better understand its place in the world, and to gain spiritual maturity? Are there ways in which non-humans could be granted enforceable rights?

23. Children's Rights
Previous generations have often made large sacrifices to provide a better life for their children. Today many of us are doing the opposite: we are sacrificing the interests of our children and their children for our own short-term comfort, believing that they will somehow find solutions to the problems we have created. In the light of this, existing children's rights agreements urgently need to be implemented, and new ones defined to insure the rights of future generations.

What sanctions for non-compliance are appropriate? How can the voice of youth be taken into account in decision-making? How can violence against children be effectively countered? Which programmes dealing with child labour and exploitation, and with supporting street children have been effective? How can the right to education receive the necessary resources? What are the best ways of restricting advertising to children? How can they best be protected from violence in the media and the Internet?

24. Science and Spirituality

Modernity rejects the super-material ('super-natural') as an impediment in the race to material prosperity. The prevailing materialistic ideology sees us only as competing genetic machines in a meaningless universe. In this atmosphere, 'scientism' has become a faith as intolerant of heretics as any religion. Materialist reductionism and social Darwinism still rule our social sciences, medicine, etc. Yet, as the study of life on ever more microscopic levels becomes possible, the evidence for its irreducible complexity and intelligence continues to grow.

Can a new dialogue between spiritual seekers and scientists overcome the increasing distrust faced by the current scientific paradigm? Could this help to create a common approach to the challenges we face? Which scientific projects should be halted until a wider consensus can be reached? Can a new social contract between science and society be established?

Endorsements for the World Future Council

"Your project is an extremely interesting one and I therefore have no objection to endorsing such an initiative. I wish you every success in this excellent undertaking."

—Boutros Boutros-Ghali, former UN Secretary General, Egypt

"The world community urgently needs long-term perspectives to improve its decision making. The WFC is filling a vital gap by emphasizing the interconnectedness and the ethical imperatives of the human enterprise."

—HRH Prince El Hassan bin Talal, Jordan

"The transition to a sustainable future is no longer a technical nor a conceptual problem; it is a problem of values, political will, and leadership. The World Future Council is designed to provide that critical leadership. I am delighted to give it my full support."

—Fritjof Capra, Scientist and Author, USA

"The World Future Council has the potential to be a very important body as part of a new framework of international governance. Future generations are not represented at the negotiations that affect their very being. The WFC will speak loudly and clearly on their behalf."

—Vandana Shiva, Director, Research Foundation for Science, Technology and Ecology, India

"To have set up the World Future Council was a timely initiative. There has never been a greater need for a body of this sort to drive home to governments and the public at large what is almost certain to be the appalling consequences of sticking for much longer to present short-sighted policies."

—Edward Goldsmith, Founder, The Ecologist, UK

"The World Future Council Initiative is one of those few rays of hope that make one feel the world might still have a future. From polices at the global level through research at the frontiers of thought level to action on the ground, each activity enriching the others, this Initiative needs the support of all those who respect the right of the next generation to have decent and fulfilling lives."

—Ashok Khosla, Director,
Centre for Development Alternatives, India

"Each human being, in his daily life, fears and hope, becomes more and more aware that beyond himself exist interests common to the whole of humankind. To face and build a viable future, we need to recognize and properly manage such a central challenge. I am pleased to welcome the World Future Council's contribution to this process which must lead to a peaceful and sustainable world."

—Georges Berthoin, Honorary Chairman of
the Jean Monnet Association, France

"The World Council for Renewable Energy welcomes the World Future Council. We are aware of the interconnectedness of energy issues with many other aspects of sustainability. The WFC is uniquely placed to help make the connections."

—Hermann Scheer, Founder, World Council for Renewable Energy;
Member of Parliament, Germany

"After 35 years of research into the positive and negative consequences of growth in industry and population, I can say without reservation, the most urgent scarcity facing humanity is the lack of long-term thinking. Most of the problems are obvious, and the solutions are clear. Action only awaits on people beginning to put long-term survival ahead of short-term material gain. The World Future Council is one of the most promising initiatives I have seen for accomplishing that."

—Dennis Meadows, Global Model Computer Analyst;
Co-Author, *Limits to Growth*, USA

"In these times when the fundamental principles of peace, justice, international law and solidarity are questioned by powerful nations and interest groups, the need for concerted action is vital and urgent. The WFC Initiative is particularly welcome as it strives to gather a global network in defence of humanistic values and in favour of concrete action. It is with great hope and conviction that I support it."

—Pierre Schori, Distinguished Visiting Professor,
Adelphi University, New York; Former UN Ambassador;
Former Minister for Development Cooperation, Sweden

"For many years I have seen the need for an organization that challenges the world community to effective action on sustainability and justice. The WFC has set its aims very high indeed and I salute its ambition to take on a big challenge."

—Dame Anita Roddick, Founder, The Body Shop, UK

"This initiative is long overdue. The fact that people of wisdom and concern for humanity are coming together under this forum is excellent news. The WFC can play a crucial role in bringing values and positive visions centre stage."

—Satish Kumar, Editor, *Resurgence* Magazine, UK

"There is an axis of evil in the world not being adequately addressed: Pandemic poverty that needlessly crushes the lives of billions of people; Unsustainable economic practices that threaten the life giving systems that bless the human community with abundance; The possession and threat to use nuclear weapons that places at risk our security and undermines our moral health.

The WFC's holisitic approach to these challenges will inspire greater public support for initiatives and policies that can make a difference."

—Jonathan Granoff, President, Global Security Institute, USA

"I welcome and support the work of the WFC Initiative. The commissions of the WFC will make a vital contribution to defining key steps towards a just and sustainable world. No other organization is currently doing this work."

—Ed Mayo, Director, Consumer Council, UK

"Long term thinking is sorely missing from the policy making process, at national, European or global levels. The WFC Initiative fills a crucial gap in the search for ways to halt and reverse the current collision course between humanity and the future."

—Caroline Lucas, Green MEP, UK

"At Friends of the Earth we welcome the broad perspective the WFC is developing. We are keenly aware that a sustainable future can only emerge as the result of the interaction of the many disciplines in which the WFC is becoming involved."

—Tony Juniper, Director, Friends of the Earth, UK

"I am delighted that the World Future Council Initiative is up and running. The WFC is a welcome colleague in the network of organizations working to fill the gap between debate and action and to build communities empowered to create change."

—Stewart Wallis, Director, New Economics Foundation, UK

"The Soil Association welcomes the creation of the World Future Council. Too many of the international community's commitments to sustainable development remain empty promises. The WFC aims to remind the world that future generations have a right to an inhabitable planet and to healthy soil on which to grow their crops. I wish it well in all its endeavours."

—Patrick Holden, Director, The Soil Association, UK

"Many people feel that progress requires us to throw off the excessive dependency on the whole complex of formal institutions which make up the over-developed, over-extended modern state. The WFC can make valuable contribution by helping people to define their own needs and to assume new, shared responsibilities."

—James Robertson, Economist and author, UK

To think—and act—in the long term implies a series of enormous changes in our behaviour and values. Precisely because I am aware of how many obstacles will have to be overcome to serve the future, I am glad that something like the World Future Council is being established. There is a lot of work to do, and hard battles to be fought.

—Luciana Castellina, Former MEP, Journalist, Italy

"The world needs the World Future Council's ethical leadership. Linking the WFC with national legislators and EarthAction's global network of civil society organizations will be a powerful combination that can help create a brighter future for all."

—Lois Barber, Executive Director, EarthAction, USA

"I have found widespread support for the World Future Council during my interviews with EarthAction partner organizations around the world. Many of these partners—in places like Malaysia, the Phillipines, Chile, Gibraltar and Albania—wish to nominate people who can share knowledge about their region and can speak with wisdom about the international issues facing us all today."

—Heidi Creamer, Researcher, EarthAction, USA

EarthAction is a global network of over 2,000 civil society organizations and national legislators in 170 countries. Since its founding in 1992, it has carried out 82 global campaigns on environment, development, peace, justice and governance issues.

In 2003, EarthAction completed two campaigns: one was on 'Stopping Child Labour', and the other focused on 'Ending Violence Against Street Children'. These campaigns involved mailing Action Kits to thousands of civil society organizations around the world, soliciting their efforts to create change through local outreach, and through influencing the actions of government officials.

Included in these mailings was information on the World Future Council Initiative. This invited organizations and individuals to endorse it and to propose WFC councillors from their region or country. In response to these mailings, organizations from 42 different countries responded and expressed their enthusiasm for the initiative. Among them were these comments:

"We support the initiative because it will create a strong voice to bridge the gap between what is being done and what needs to be done."

—Joseph Mukasa, Director, Association for Country-Wide
Afforestation: Environment and Development, Uganda

"At a juncture when the human population exploits the resource ensemble of the earth and endangers the ecological matrix of life, the World Future Council may substantially contribute to a better quality of life in the 21st century."

—Dr. Ram Vilas Verma, Institute for
Regional Development Studies, India

"The WFC will address the current global crisis by sharing positive ideas and taking initiatives. Current global crises could be very well addressed and bring solutions to the limelight by coming together from all parts of the world."

—Joseph Kennedy Kogo Afful, Amazing Saving Grace, Ghana

"A noble idea and cause towards a better world for mankind. May we live to see the dream come true."

—Charles Maina Kariuki, Global Goodwill
Community Centre, Kenya

"This initiative is a very laudable one that calls for our collective commitment and hard work. It will succeed."

—Chris N. Ugwu, Nigeria Society for the
Improvement of Rural People, Nigeria

Many eminent people from around the world endorse the World Future Council Initiative, and they include the following:

Franco Amurri, Film Director, Italy

Uri and Rachel Avnery, Founders, Gush Salom, Israel

Rajni Bakshi, Journalist, India

Serge Beddington Behrens, Psychotherapist, UK

Barbara Fields Bernstein, Co-founder, The Association for Global New Thought, USA

Rosalie Bertell, President, International Institute of Concern for Public Health, Canada

Moyra Bremner, Author, TV journalist, UK

James Bruges, Author, UK

Dora Buyamukama, Member of Parliament, Uganda

Daniele Capezzone, Secretary-General, Radical Party, Italy

Guiseppe Cassini, Ambassador, Italy

Sheshrao Chavan, Author, Chairman, Institute of World Problems, India

Giulietto Chiesa, Writer, TV Producer, Italy

Armand Clesse, Director, Institute for European and International Studies, Luxembourg

Barry Coates, Executive Director, Oxfam New Zealand

Andrew Cohen, Founder of *What Is Enlightenment* Magazine, USA

Stephen Corry, Director, Survival International, UK

Guy Dauncey, Founder, The Solutions Project, Canada

Kristin Dawkins, President, Institute for Agriculture and Trade Policy, USA

Roberto Della Seta, President, Legambiente, Italy

Demba Moussa Dembele, Director, Forum for African Alternatives, Senegal

Felix Dodds, Executive Director, Stakeholder Forum for Our Common Future, UK

Hans-Peter Duerr, Scientist, Max Planck Institute, Germany
Nicholas Dunlop, Secretary General, E-Parliament Initiative, UK
Olivier Dupuis, MEP, Transnational Radical Party, Italy
Scilla Elworthy, Director, Peace Direct, UK
Tewolde Berhan Gebre Egziabher, General Manager, Environmental
    Protection Authority, Ethiopia
Samuel Epstein, Founder, Cancer Prevention Coalition, London
Romy Fraser, Director, Neal's Yard Remedies, London
Johan Galtung, Author, Peace Researcher, Norway
Ela Gandhi, Member of Parliament, South Africa
Maneka Gandhi, Member of Parliament, India
Jim Garrison, President, State of the World Forum, USA
Stephen Gaskin, Co-Founder, Plenty International, USA
Robley E. George, Director, Centre for the Study of Democratic
    Societies, USA
Susan George, Transnational Institute, France
Olivier Giscard d'Estaing, Chairman, COPAM, France
Thomas Grunert, Head of Division, European Parliament, Belgium
Prabhu Guptara, Director, Wolfsberg Executive Development
    Centre, Switzerland
Teresa Hale, Founder, Hale Clinic, UK
Eirwen Harbottle, Director, Centre for International Peace-Building,
    UK
Liz Hosken, Director, Gaia Foundation, UK
Denis Hayes, President, The Bullitt Foundation, USA
Cyd Ho, Member of the Legislative Council, Hong Kong
Kamil Hossain, Chair, Centre for International Sustainable
    Development Law, USA
S. M. Mohammed Idris, Sahabat Alam, Malaysia
Maria Ivanova, Director, Global Environmental Governance Project,
    USA
Wes Jackson, Founder, The Land Institute, USA
Richard Jolly, Former Acting Director, UNICEF

Tony Juniper, Director, Friends of the Earth, UK
J. C. Kapur, Editor, World Affairs, India
Martin Khor, Director, Third World Network, Malaysia
Maritta Koch-Weser, President, Earth3000, Germany
Ervin Laszlo, President, The Club of Budapest, Hungary
Ian Lee, One World Healing Foundation, UK
Bernard Lietaer, Chairman, ACCESS Foundation, USA
David Lorimer, Founder, Medical and Scientific Network, UK
J. Steven Lovink, Co-Founder, The Institute of Environmental
    Security, USA
Barbara Marx Hubbard, Founder, Foundation for Conscious
    Evolution, USA
Niels Meyer, Professor of Physics, Technical University,
    Copenhagen, Denmark
Helena Norberg-Hodge, Founder, International Society for Ecology
    & Culture, UK
Sirpa Pietikäinen, President, World Federation of UN Associations,
    Finland
Andrei Piontkovsky, Director, Centre for Strategic Studies, Russia
Joseph Rotblat, Nobel Peace Prize Laureate, UK
Jonathon Porritt, Programme Director, Forum for the Future, UK
Samuel Kojo Quansah, Executive Director, International Christian
    Fellowship Association for Child Care, Ghana
Wolfgang Sachs, Senior Research Fellow, Wuppertal Institute,
    Germany
Elisabeth Sahtouris, Evolution Biologist, Author, Business
    Consultant
Ziauddin Sardar, Editor, *Futures*, UK
Diana Schumacher, Former President, Schumacher Society, UK
David Shreeve, Co-Founder, Conservation Foundation, UK
Brijraj Singh, Maharawal of Jaiselmer, India
Gaj Singh, Maharawal of Jodhpur, India

Robin Stott, Chairman, Medical Peace and Environment Group, UK
Andrew Strauss, Widener University, School of Law, USA
Vinod Tailor, Trustee, Hamare Apne, UK
Richard Toledo-Leyva, Oficina para Estudios de Riesgos
    Catastroficos, Mexico
Steven Trevino, Chief Strategist, Global Sustainability, ASE, Inc.,
    USA
William Ury, Director, Harvard University Global Negotiation
    Project, USA
Theo van Boven, Ex-Director, UN Division for Human Rights,
    Netherlands
Wouter van Dieren, IMSA Environmental Consult & Innovation,
    Netherlands
Ernst von Weizsaecker, Member of Parliament, Germany
Susan Witt, Executive Director, E. F. Schumacher Society, USA
David and Rosey Woollcombe, Peace Child International, UK
Derek Wyatt, Member of Parliament, UK